WE ARE THE CHAMPIONS
NCAA BASKETBALL CHAMPIONSHIP

Annalise Bekkering

AV² provides enriched content that supplements and complements this book. Weigl's AV² books strive to create inspired learning and engage young minds in a total learning experience.

Your AV² Media Enhanced books come alive with...

Audio
Listen to sections of the book read aloud.

Key Words
Study vocabulary, and complete a matching word activity.

Video
Watch informative video clips.

Quizzes
Test your knowledge.

Embedded Weblinks
Gain additional information for research.

Slide Show
View images and captions, and prepare a presentation.

Try This!
Complete activities and hands-on experiments.

... and much, much more!

Go to **www.av2books.com**, and enter this book's unique code.

BOOK CODE

AVU85695

AV² by Weigl brings you media enhanced books that support active learning.

Published by AV² by Weigl
350 5th Avenue, 59th Floor
New York, NY 10118
Website: www.av2books.com

Library of Congress Cataloging-in-Publication Data

Names: Bekkering, Annalise, author.
Title: NCAA basketball championship / Annalise Bekkering.
Other titles: National Collegiate Athletic Association basketball championship
Description: New York, NY : AV² by Weigl, 2020. | Series: We are the champions | Includes index. | Audience: K to Grade 3.
Identifiers: LCCN 2018055400 (print) | LCCN 2018060002 (ebook) | ISBN 9781791100391 (Multi User ebook) | ISBN 9781791100407 (Single User ebook) | ISBN 9781791100384 (hardcover : alk. paper) | ISBN 9781791105808 (softcover : alk. paper)
Subjects: LCSH: NCAA Basketball Tournament--Juvenile literature.
Classification: LCC GV885.49.N37 (ebook) | LCC GV885.49.N37 B46 2020 (print) | DDC 796.323/630973--dc23
LC record available at https://lccn.loc.gov/2018055400

Printed in Brainerd, Minnesota, United States
1 2 3 4 5 6 7 8 9 0   22 21 20 19 18

122018
102318

Project Coordinator: Jared Siemens
Art Director: Terry Paulhus

Every reasonable effort has been made to trace ownership and to obtain permission to reprint copyright material. The publishers would be pleased to have any errors or omissions brought to their attention so that they may be corrected in subsequent printings. Weigl acknowledges Getty Images, Newscom, and Alamy as its primary image suppliers for this title.

WE ARE THE CHAMPIONS
NCAA BASKETBALL CHAMPIONSHIP

CONTENTS

3

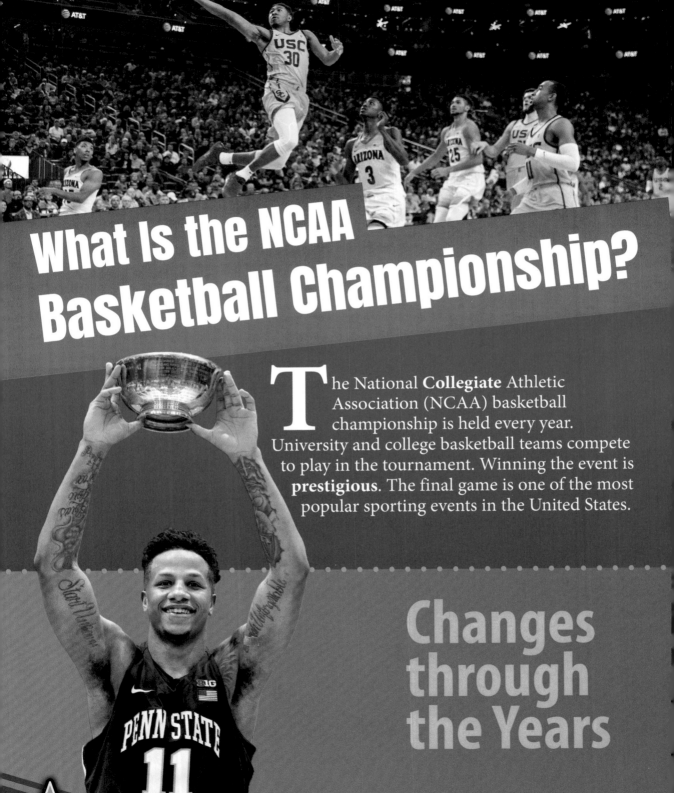

What Is the NCAA Basketball Championship?

The National **Collegiate** Athletic Association (NCAA) basketball championship is held every year. University and college basketball teams compete to play in the tournament. Winning the event is **prestigious**. The final game is one of the most popular sporting events in the United States.

Changes through the Years

The NCAA oversees most college and university sports in the United States. More than 1,000 schools are members of the NCAA. Member schools are divided into three divisions. Division I is made up of the largest schools.

Division II and Division III schools are smaller. All three divisions host championship games. The Division I championship is the most popular. All of the athletes that compete in the NCAA are students. They have academic responsibilities to maintain. Athletes must achieve high grades to be able to play sports for their school.

On game days, Division I school arenas are filled with fans. Many are current students who come to cheer on their peers. Many others are simply fans of the game, thrilled by the excitement and energy generated by teams competing for a chance to win the NCAA Championship.

Only about **1 percent** of NCAA players go on to play major professional basketball.

There are **353** men's teams and **351** women's teams competing in Division I basketball.

There are more than **180,000** student-athletes participating in Division I sports.

PAST

In 1939, there was an audience of 5,500 people for the final game.

In 1977, the average ticket price was $7.78.

In 1946, about 500,000 people watched the final game on television.

In 1985, the shot clock was set at 45 seconds.

PRESENT

In 2018, the final game was attended by 67,831 fans.

The average ticket price for the championship game was $1,110 in 2018.

In 2017, close to 23 million people watched the championship game on television.

In 2015, the shot clock was reduced to 30 seconds.

The History

Dr. James Naismith invented basketball in 1891, in Springfield, Massachusetts. He created the game for students to play inside during the winter. The game was played with a soccer ball. Peach baskets were hung at each end of the gymnasium. Players would climb up a ladder to get the ball from the baskets. The bottom of the baskets was cut out so the ball would fall to the ground.

Basketball became popular very quickly. The first college game with five players on each side was played in 1896. The University of Chicago beat the University of Iowa 15–12. About 90 colleges in the United States had basketball teams by 1900.

The Intercollegiate Athletic Association of the United States (IAAUS) formed in 1906. The organization was created to oversee college sports. It became the National Collegiate Athletic Association (NCAA) four years later. More than 360 colleges had basketball teams by 1914.

James Naismith coached the first basketball team at the University of Kansas in 1891.

The first national basketball tournament was hosted in Kansas City, Missouri, in 1937. However, all the teams came from the Midwest instead of from across the nation. The National Invitational Tournament (NIT) held its first event in 1938. The tournament was held in New York. It received attention across the country. The first NCAA tournament was held the following year. It was organized by the National Association of Basketball Coaches (NABC). They wanted to bring more attention to basketball in the western states. Over time, the NCAA attracted the sport's top teams and the NIT became less and less popular. In 2005, the NCAA purchased the NIT. The NIT has continued as a second-tier competition for Division I basketball.

NCAA basketball had eight districts for the first 12 years. One team from each district played in the basketball tournament. The NCAA tournament has grown to include 68 teams. The NCAA basketball championship is also called March Madness. It is one of the biggest sporting events in the United States.

Bill Russell is only one of seven players in the "Triple Crown Club," players who have won a championship in the NCAA, NBA, and Olympics.

BASKETBALL CHEERS

Basketball fans have different chants and cheers for their favorite teams. Many universities have a school song. These songs are part of a school tradition. The University of Ohio song is called "Stand Up and Cheer."

The Rules

Basketball rules have changed since the sport was invented in 1891. Rules are added and adapted over time to keep the game fair and players safe. Some leagues have different rules, but the game is similar wherever it is played.

1

The Game

NCAA basketball games have two halves. Each half is 20 minutes. There is a 15-minute break between halves. This is called halftime. The team with the highest score at the end of the game wins. If the score is tied at the end of the game, the teams play five minutes of overtime. Each team is allowed five players on the court at once. These five players play **offense** and **defense**.

2

Beginning the Game

Every basketball game begins with a jump ball. A player from each team faces off at center court. The other players line up around the circle at center. A referee tosses the ball in the air. The two players in the middle jump and try to knock the ball to one of their teammates.

3

Moving the Ball

There are two ways to move the basketball around the court. They are dribbling and passing. Dribbling is done by bouncing the ball against the floor. Players must dribble the ball to move around the court. If a player takes a step while holding the ball, it is called traveling. This is against the rules. Basketball players pass to their teammates by throwing the ball through the air. They can also bounce the ball to their teammates.

4

Scoring

A team scores points by shooting the ball into the basket. A team scores two points for a shot taken close to the hoop. A team scores three points for a shot from behind the **three-point line**. The offensive team has 30 seconds to shoot the ball at the net in NCAA basketball. The defensive team tries to stop the other team from scoring. They try to block shots and passes. They can also try to steal control of the ball.

5

Fouls

The referee calls a foul when there is illegal contact between players. A foul can be called for pushing, tripping, or holding. If an offensive player is fouled while shooting, they get to take a foul shot. The player stands at a special place on the court called the free-throw line. A foul shot is worth one point. A player can also get a technical foul for unsportsmanlike behavior.

MAKING THE CALL

There are three referees for NCAA basketball games. They make sure players are following the rules. A referee must know all of the rules of basketball. The referee stops the game by blowing a whistle when a rule is broken. Referees run up and down the court to watch the players. A referee must be able to make decisions very quickly.

The Basketball Court

Basketball is played on a rectangular court. Outdoor courts are usually asphalt or concrete. Indoor courts often have hardwood floors or are made out of flexible, interlocking tiles. It is 94 feet (28.7 meters) long by 50 feet (15.2 m) wide. There is a basket at each end of the court. The basket is 18 inches (45.7 centimeters) in diameter. The backboard behind the basket is 3.5 or 4 feet (1.1 or 1.2 m) high by 6 feet (1.8 m) wide.

There is a rectangular box drawn on the floor at each end of the court. In NCAA basketball, this box is 19 feet (5.8 m) long by 12 feet (3.7 m) wide. This area is called the key. Offensive players are only allowed to stand in the key for three seconds. The free-throw line is at the top of the key. It is 15 feet (4.6 m) from the backboard. The three-point line in NCAA basketball is an **arced** line 20 feet and 9 inches (6.3 m) from the basket. Any shot made from behind this line is worth three points.

PLAYERS ON THE TEAM

Each basketball team has five players on the court at one time. Each member of the team has different strengths and skills. All teammates play both offense and defense. On offense, the point guard is usually small and fast, and has excellent ball handling and passing skills. The shooting guard is often very quick, and is good at scoring and passing. The small forward is good at scoring both near and far from the net. The power forward is normally big and strong. This player needs good defensive and **rebounding** skills. The center is usually the tallest player on the team. Centers score many points near the net and block shots on defense. The coach is an important part of the team. This person is in charge of strategy and instructing players.

BASKETBALL COURT

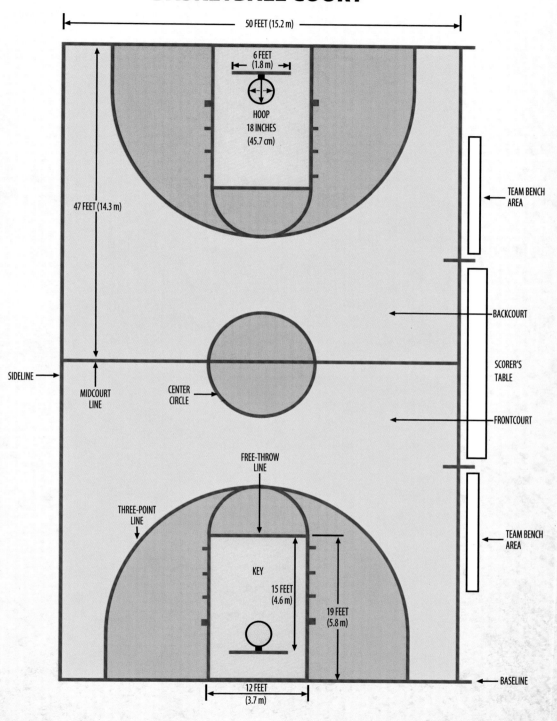

50 FEET (15.2 m)

6 FEET
(1.8 m)

HOOP
18 INCHES
(45.7 cm)

TEAM BENCH
AREA

47 FEET (14.3 m)

BACKCOURT

SCORER'S
TABLE

SIDELINE

MIDCOURT
LINE

CENTER
CIRCLE

FRONTCOURT

FREE-THROW
LINE

THREE-POINT
LINE

TEAM BENCH
AREA

KEY

15 FEET
(4.6 m)

19 FEET
(5.8 m)

12 FEET
(3.7 m)

BASELINE

The Equipment

Playing basketball requires very little equipment. This is one of the reasons it is such a popular sport. People of different ages and skill levels can play basketball.

The most important piece of equipment is a basketball. The ball is usually made of nylon or leather, and is orange or brown in color. The surface of the ball is pebbled. This rough surface allows players to grip the ball. A men's basketball is 29.5 to 30 inches (74.9 to 76.2 cm) in **circumference** and weighs 20 to 22 ounces (567 to 624 grams).

Most players wear high-top shoes. Basketball players move around a lot and make quick movements from side to side. Having high-top shoes helps prevent players from injuring their ankles.

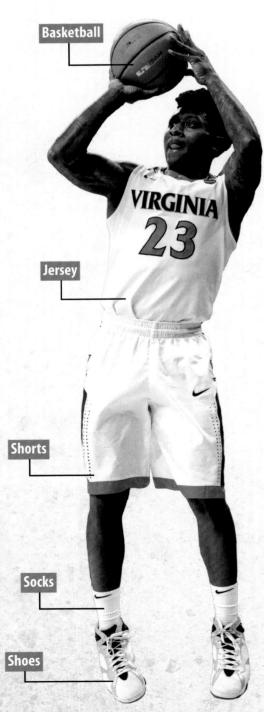

Basketball

Jersey

Shorts

Socks

Shoes

The basket is another important piece of equipment. The rim is made out of metal and has a diameter of 18 inches (45.7 cm). The net below is made from nylon. In outdoor basketball, the net is sometimes made out of chains. The basket is attached to a backboard made of plastic or glass. Sometimes players try to bounce the ball off the backboard to get the ball to fall into the basket.

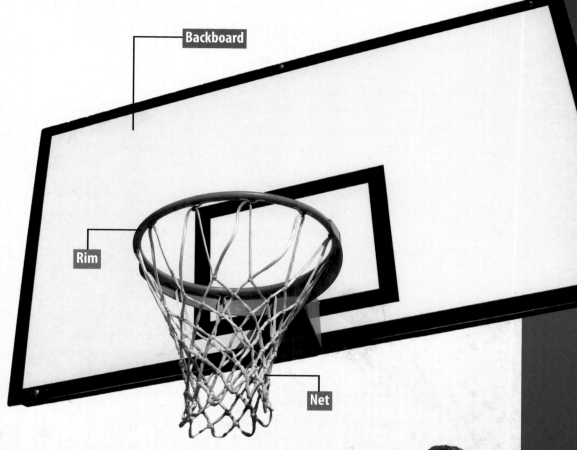

Backboard

Rim

Net

TEAM UNIFORMS

Most basketball uniforms have a sleeveless top and shorts in the team's colors. The uniforms are made out of synthetic, or man-made, materials, such as nylon, polyester, or rayon. Players have a number on the front and back of their uniform. In the NCAA, the players can have the numbers 00, 0 to 5, 10 to 15, 20 to 25, 30 to 35, 40 to 45, or 50 to 55. Sometimes, the player's last name is written on the back of the uniform above the number. In the NCAA, each team has a light-colored uniform and a dark-colored uniform. The home team wears the light uniform. The visiting team wears the dark uniform.

Qualifying to Play

The Division I final tournament is called the Final Four. The road to the Final Four takes place over three weeks in March and April every year. Sixty-eight teams qualify for the NCAA championship tournament. The selection of these teams is a complicated process. There are 32 **conferences** in the NCAA that automatically have one team qualify for the championship tournament. Every conference has its own tournament. Each winning team qualifies as one of the 68 teams to play in the NCAA championship tournament. A committee selects the remaining 36 teams. They try to choose the country's best teams for the tournament.

The committee chooses eight of the lowest ranked teams to play against each other. This round of games is called the First Four. The four winning teams of the First Four move on to the first round of the NCAA tournament. The committee arranges the teams in a **bracket**. The bracket determines which teams will play each other based on region and rank.

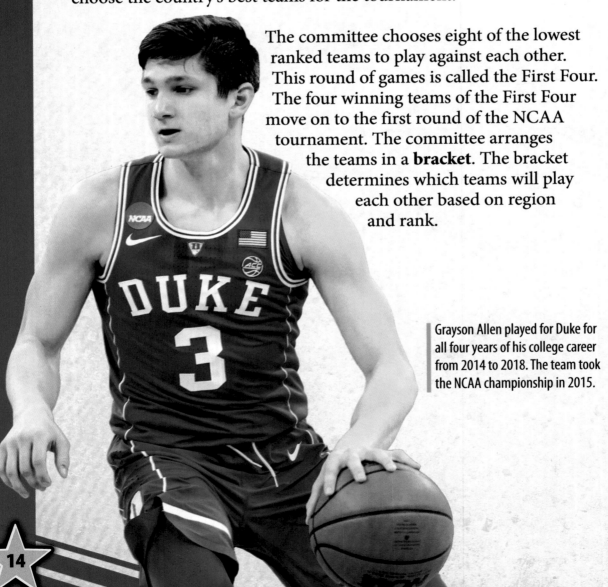

Grayson Allen played for Duke for all four years of his college career from 2014 to 2018. The team took the NCAA championship in 2015.

The Kansas Jayhawks have made 47 tournament appearances, including the Final Four in 2018.

In the first round, there are four regional tournaments of 16 teams each. The four regions are East, West, South, and Midwest. In each region, the highest-ranked teams play against the lowest-ranked teams. Once a team loses a game, it is out of the competition. The winning teams move on to the next round.

There are 32 teams in the second round of the tournament. Each team plays another team, and the winners move on to the next round. Winners continue playing each other until there are only four teams left in the tournament. These four teams are the regional champions. They play in the national semifinals, known as the Final Four. The winners of this round play each other for the championship.

THE NET

Cutting down the net is an NCAA tradition for the championship team. Each player from the winning team cuts a piece of the basketball net. The coach cuts the last piece. Each player keeps a small piece of the net as a souvenir, and the coach keeps the rest.

The Main Event

The NCAA basketball championship game is a major event. Many cities compete for the opportunity to host the Final Four. The first NCAA tournament was held at Patten Gymnasium in Evanston, Illinois. The national championship game has been played in Kansas City, Missouri, more times than any other city. It has been played there 10 times. The biggest crowd for an NCAA championship final was in 2014 in Dallas. There were 79,238 people there to watch the University of Connecticut defeat Kentucky 60–54.

The host city is chosen a few years in advance. This gives the city time to prepare for the big event. The Final Four event draws large crowds. Since 1997, every championship series has been played in a football dome stadium instead of a basketball arena in order to accommodate more people.

Ohio is the only state to have **two teams** compete for the final game. Cincinnati beat Ohio State in 1961.

In 2018, the state of Texas had a record **seven** teams invited to the NCAA tournament.

The Villanova University Wildcats have played in **38** NCAA tournaments, 6 Final Fours, and claimed 3 championships.

The Louisville Cardinals won the 2013 NCAA Championship with the help of forward Luke Hancock. Hancock scored 22 points in the final game against the Michigan Wolverines.

5 YEARS
OF NCAA CHAMPIONS

WINNING TEAM	SCORE	LOSING TEAM
2018 Villanova	 79-62	**2018** Michigan
2017 North Carolina	 71-65	**2017** Gonzaga
2016 Villanova	 77-74	**2016** North Carolina
2015 Duke	 68-63	**2015** Wisconsin
2014 Connecticut	 60-54	**2014** Kentucky

NCAA TROPHIES

The NCAA championship-winning team receives two trophies. One trophy is gold-plated. It is a National Championship trophy awarded by the NCAA. The other trophy is from the National Association of Basketball Coaches. It is made out of Waterford crystal. This trophy is shaped like a basketball.

Where They Play

There are 351 NCAA Division I schools in the United States. Use the map and legend to see which NCAA Division I champions are from schools near you.

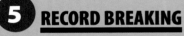

5 RECORD BREAKING

The Carrier Dome at Syracuse University in New York has been setting on-campus attendance records since it was built in 1980. In 2014, it hosted a record-breaking 35,446 fans for a game between Syracuse and Duke, which Syracuse won in overtime.

NCAA Division I Champions Since 1967

1 University of Kansas – 1988, 2008
2 University of Florida – 2006, 2007
3 University of North Carolina – 1982, 1993, 2005, 2009, 2017
4 University of Connecticut – 1999, 2004, 2011, 2014

5 Syracuse University – 2003
6 University of Maryland – 2002
7 Duke University – 1991, 1992, 2001, 2010, 2015
8 Michigan State University – 1979, 2000
9 University of Kentucky – 1978, 1996, 1998, 2012
10 University of Arizona – 1997

CANADA

North Dakota

Minnesota

South Dakota

Wisconsin

Iowa

Nebraska

Illinois

Indiana

Ohio

Michigan

Maine

New Hampshire

Vermont

Massachusetts

Rhode Island

Connecticut

New York

Pennsylvania

New Jersey

Delaware

Maryland

District of Columbia

Virginia

West Virginia

Missouri

Kansas

Oklahoma

Arkansas

Kentucky

Tennessee

North Carolina

South Carolina

Texas

Louisiana

Alabama

Georgia

Florida

Atlantic Ocean

MAP LEGEND

- ☐ United States
- ☐ Other Countries
- ☐ Water
- **#** NCAA Division I Champions

SCALE

0 miles — 360 miles

0 kilometers — 580 km

11 UCLA – 1967, 1968, 1969, 1970, 1971, 1972, 1973, 1975, 1995

12 University of Arkansas – 1994

13 UNLV – 1990

14 University of Michigan – 1989

15 Indiana University – 1976, 1981, 1987

16 University of Louisville – 1980, 1986, 2013

17 Villanova University – 1985, 2016, 2018

18 Georgetown University – 1984

19 North Carolina State University – 1974, 1983

20 Marquette University – 1977

19

Women in Basketball

At first, women's basketball was not a popular sport. In 1892, women's basketball had its own set of rules. Women played the first basketball tournament using men's rules in 1926. The first five-player, full-court women's game was played in 1971.

In 1972, the government passed a law called Title IX. This rule said schools had to fund men's and women's sports equally. Women's sports programs began to grow. In 1978, the Association for Intercollegiate Athletics for Women (AIAW) televised their championship. The Women's Basketball League (WBL), a women's professional league, was also formed that year.

The number of girls competing in high school sports also increased. By 1972, about 2.7 percent of girls participated in school sports. Today, more than 50 percent of girls participate in school sports.

The AIAW ended in 1982 and the NCAA took control of women's college sports. That year, Louisiana Tech defeated Cheyney State 76–62, to win the first NCAA Division I Women's Basketball championship.

Before going to the Women's National Basketball Association, Kim Williams played college basketball for DePaul University from 1995 to 1997.

Women's basketball became very popular in the 1990s. The Women's National Basketball Association (WNBA) was formed in 1996. This league gives top female college players the opportunity to play professional basketball in the United States.

Today, women's basketball is played with the same rules as men's basketball. There are a few differences. A smaller ball is used in women's games. Also, the three-point line is one foot closer to the basket in women's NCAA games than in men's NCAA games.

Millions of fans watch the women's NCAA championship every year. The championship follows the same format as the men's tournament.

Caitlin Jenkins joined Rutgers University for the 2017–18 season, averaging 5.2 points and 7.7 rebounds per game.

DIANA TAURASI

Diana Taurasi had one of the most successful college careers in women's basketball. She played for the University of Connecticut for four years from 2000 to 2004. Her team won the NCAA championship three of those years. In college, Taurasi averaged 15 points, 4.5 assists, and 4.3 rebounds per game. She was named the Naismith National Player of the Year in 2003 and 2004. Taurasi was the first draft pick in the 2004 WNBA draft. She currently plays for the Phoenix Mercury. In 2017, she became the WNBA's all-time leading scorer.

Important Moments

Some of the greatest basketball players in the world have played in the NCAA basketball championship. These players have created memorable moments in the tournament. Some championship games have been won and lost in the final seconds.

The term "March Madness" was first used in 1939 by H. V. Porter to describe the Illinois high school basketball finals. The term began to be used for the NCAA championship tournament in the 1980s.

Beginning in 1962, coach John Wooden led UCLA to 12 Final Four tournaments in 14 years. His team won the championship 10 times. UCLA won the NCAA championship seven years in a row from 1967 to 1973.

In 1979, Earvin "Magic" Johnson and Michigan State defeated Larry Bird and Indiana State in the NCAA championship. Magic Johnson and Larry Bird both went on to become superstars in the National Basketball Association (NBA).

In 1983, the North Carolina State Wolfpack played the University of Houston in the championship game. Houston was favored to win, and North Carolina State was the **underdog**. In the final few seconds of the game, Lorenzo Charles of North Carolina State made a surprise basket. He scored a **slam dunk**, and the Wolfpack won the game 54–52.

After four years with Syracuse, Hakim Warrick joined the NBA in 2005.

In the 2003 championship game, Kansas was down by three points to Syracuse. With only two seconds left, Michael Lee of Kansas took a shot from the three-point line. Hakim Warrick of Syracuse blocked the ball and knocked it out of bounds. Syracuse won 81–78.

In the 2015–16 final game against North Carolina, Villanova won with a three-pointer by forward Kris Jenkins, just as time ran out. In 2018, Villanova took home the trophy for the second time in three years, with a 79–62 win against the Michigan Wolverines.

NCAA BASKETBALL TOURNAMENT RECORDS

44
Points, Final Game
Bill Walton
1973

94
Tournament Game
Wins by a Coach
Mike Krzyzewski

11
Three-point Field
Goals, Single Game
Jeff Fryer
1990

61
Points, Single Game
Austin Carr
1970

34
Rebounds,
Single Game
Fred Cohen
1956

18
Assists, Final Four
Single Game
Mark Wade
1987

11
Blocked Shots,
Single Game
Shaquille O'Neal
1992

58
Points, Final Four
Single Game
Bill Bradley
1965

Legends and Current Stars

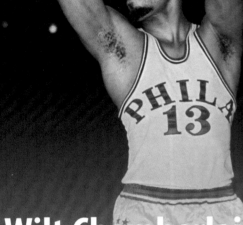

Wilt Chamberlain
Center

Wilt Chamberlain attended the University of Kansas and played for the Jayhawks from 1956 to 1959. He averaged 29.9 points and 18.3 rebounds per game during his college career. Because Chamberlain was more than 7 feet (213 cm) tall, the NCAA added rules so that he did not have an advantage over other players. Chamberlain never won an NCAA championship. In his sophomore year, his team lost the championship in triple overtime. Although his team lost, Chamberlain was named the most valuable player (MVP) of the tournament. Chamberlain played professional basketball in the NBA from 1959 to 1973. He won two NBA championships and set many records. In one game, he scored 100 points. This remains the highest individual score in NBA history. Chamberlain ended his basketball career in 1973. He passed away in 1999.

Michael Jordan
Guard

Michael Jordan is one of basketball's most recognizable players. He played for the University of North Carolina Tar Heels from 1981 to 1984. Jordan is known for one of the most memorable moments in NCAA championship history. In the 1982 NCAA championship game, he made a **jump shot** in the last second of the game to defeat Georgetown University 63-62. After college, Jordan spent many years playing for the Chicago Bulls in the NBA. He led the Bulls to six NBA championships and won six MVP awards. Jordan first retired from basketball in 1998. He returned to play two seasons with the Washington Wizards from 2001 to 2003, before retiring again.

24

Mario Chalmers
Guard

Mario Chalmers played for the University of Kansas Jayhawks from 2005 to 2008. He helped lead his team to the NCAA championship title in 2008. He was named the Most Outstanding Player of the Final Four that year. Chalmers is an extraordinary defensive player. In his final year with the team, he had 97 steals and 169 assists. Chalmers is known for one of the most memorable plays in the NCAA championships. In the 2008 championship game against Memphis, he made a three-point shot with 2.1 seconds left, tying the game. His team then won in overtime. Chalmers joined the NBA in 2008 when he was drafted by the Miami Heat. He helped the Heat win the NBA championship in 2012. In 2015, Chalmers transferred to the Memphis Grizzlies.

Carmelo Anthony
Forward

Carmelo Anthony played one year of college basketball. In the 2002–03 season, he led Syracuse University to its first-ever NCAA championship victory. He set the school record for points by a freshman in a season with 778 points, and set the Big East Conference record for points per game by a rookie at 22.5. In the championship game versus Kansas, Anthony had 20 points, 10 rebounds, and seven assists. Syracuse won the game 81-78. Anthony was named the tournament's most valuable player. He was the third freshman to win the award. Anthony has played for the Denver Nuggets, New York Knicks, Oklahoma City Thunder, and Houston Rockets, who he started playing for in 2018, in his 17-year career. He has been one of the top-10 point scorers in nine of those seasons and has been named an All-Star twelve times.

138

Grinnell College's Jack Taylor scored a record number of points in a single game in 2012.

3,667

Pete Maravich holds the NCAA record for most career points from his time with Louisiana State University in the 1960s.

13

Before he joined the Brooklyn Nets, Mookie Blaylock played for the University of Oklahoma, where he holds the record for steals in a single game. He set the record twice, once in 1987 and again in 1988.

16

In 2007, Mickell Gladness of Alabama A&M University made the most blocks in a single game. He played for the NBA for one season, 2011–12.

982

Tyler Hansbrough made a record number of free throws over his four years playing for the University of North Carolina.

NCAA Basketball Championship Timeline

1950   **1960**   **1970**

S tudent-athletes have been meeting on the court to determine basketball dominance since the first college basketball program was developed more than 100 years ago. Each year, new rosters of players continue to test themselves, striving to claim the NCAA basketball championship.

1953
The tournament expands from 16 to 22 teams.

1966
Texas Western University wins the championship. They are the first team with an all–African American starting lineup.

1954
The NCAA championship game is televised nationally for the first time.

1939
The first NCAA championship takes place. The University of Oregon wins the championship.

1975
The tournament expands to 32 teams.

1985
The tournament expands to 64 teams. Villanova, the eighth-**seeded** team, becomes the lowest-seeded team to ever win the NCAA championship.

2011
The NCAA tournament expands to 68 teams. No first-seeded teams make it to the Final Four. It is only the second time this has happened since the tournament expanded to 53 teams in 1984.

1980 **1990** **2000** **2010** **TODAY**

1966
UCLA's coach John Wooden leads his team to the first of seven NCAA championship titles in a row. About 39 million people watch the championship game on television.

2001
The tournament expands to 65 teams. Almost 16 million people watch the televised championship game.

2018
The NCAA announces new rule changes to help college players, allowing players to hire agents and return to college if they do not make it past a certain stage of the NBA draft process.

1 Who invented the game of basketball?

2 Which team won the first NCAA championship?

3 In 2011, the NCAA tournament expanded to how many teams?

4 How many NCAA Division I schools are there in the United States?

5 What university team did Michael Jordan play for?

10 QUESTIONS To Test Your Knowledge

6 How many referees are there in an NCAA basketball game?

7 Which was the first team with an all–African American starting lineup?

8 What is the name of the first round of games in the NCAA tournament?

9 Who holds the record for blocked shots in a single NCAA tournament game?

10 Which is the lowest-seeded team to ever win the NCAA championship?

ANSWERS
1. Dr. James Naismith
2. University of Oregon
3. 68
4. 351
5. University of North Carolina Tar Heels
6. Three
7. Texas Western University
8. The First Four
9. Shaquille O'Neal
10. Villanova in 1985

Key Words

arced: curved, like an arch

bracket: a diagram showing a series of games in a tournament

circumference: the distance around an object

collegiate: having to do with college or college students

conferences: groups of sports teams

defense: the team that is trying to keep another team from scoring

jump shot: a shot that is made while the player is jumping

offense: the team that has the ball and is trying to score points

prestigious: having high status and a good reputation

rebounding: grabbing the ball after it bounces off the rim or the backboard

seeded: how a team is ranked in a tournament

slam dunk: a shot made when the player stuffs the ball through the basket

three-point line: a half circle around the center of the basket

underdog: the team with a disadvantage that is expected to lose

Index

Log on to www.av2books.com

AV² by Weigl brings you media enhanced books that support active learning. Go to www.av2books.com, and enter the special code found on page 2 of this book. You will gain access to enriched and enhanced content that supplements and complements this book. Content includes video, audio, weblinks, quizzes, a slide show, and activities.

AV² Online Navigation

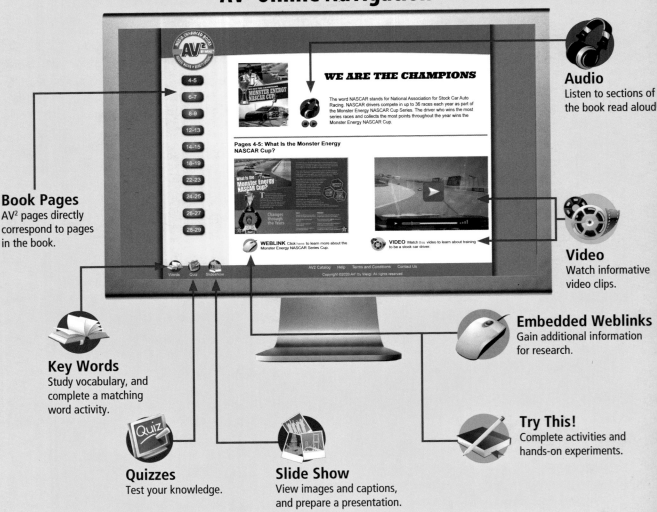

Audio
Listen to sections of the book read aloud

Book Pages
AV² pages directly correspond to pages in the book.

Video
Watch informative video clips.

Embedded Weblinks
Gain additional information for research.

Key Words
Study vocabulary, and complete a matching word activity.

Try This!
Complete activities and hands-on experiments.

Quizzes
Test your knowledge.

Slide Show
View images and captions, and prepare a presentation.

AV² was built to bridge the gap between print and digital. We encourage you to tell us what you like and what you want to see in the future.

Sign up to be an AV² Ambassador at www.av2books.com/ambassador.